W0032712

ELISABETH

Bilder einer Kaiserin
Portraits of an Empress

Frohe Weihnacht 1992
HABASIT GmbH, Wien

Elisabeth

Bilder einer Kaiserin
Portraits of an Empress

Herausgegeben von Brigitte Hamann

Amalthea

© 1986 by Amalthea-Verlag, Wien–München
Engl. Übersetzung: Megan W. Schmidt
Alle Rechte vorbehalten
Layout: Adolf Pallanch
Satz: Rudolf Schaber, Wels
Gesamtherstellung: Wiener Verlag, Himberg bei Wien
Printed in Austria 1986
ISBN 3-85002-156-4

Inhalt · Contents

Vorwort · Introduction	6
Ein Kind in Bayern · A Child in Bavaria	8
Die Braut · The Bride	14
Hochzeit in Wien · The Marriage in Vienna	22
Die junge Mutter · The Young Mother	36
Krankheit und Flucht · Illness and Escape	42
Porträts · Portraits	48
Königin von Ungarn · The Queen of Hungary	84
Repräsentation · Representation	100
Trösterin der Armen · Comforter of the Poor	124
Die Reiterin · The Equestrian	130
Familienleben · Family Life	144
Titanias Weltflucht · Titania's Flight from the World	162
Bildnachweis · Origin of Pictures	184

Vorwort

Wenn wir die fast dreihundert Bilder der Kaiserin Elisabeth in diesem Buch gesehen haben: Sind wir dann ihrer Person nähergekommen? Können wir sie uns wirklich vorstellen?

Um keine falschen Erwartungen zu wecken, gleich anfangs die Antwort: Nein. Die Persönlichkeit der Kaiserin Elisabeth ist zwar in ihren Briefen, ihren Gedichten erkennbar, nicht aber in den vielen Porträts und Darstellungen, die die Künstler von ihr anfertigten. Diese Bilder dokumentieren die Legendengestalt namens Sisi, so wie die Zeitgenossen sie gesehen haben und sehen wollten. Die so überaus spannungsreiche, widersprüchliche Frau Elisabeth bleibt weitgehend verborgen.

An dieser Tatsache sind freilich die Künstler unschuldig. Die Kaiserin selbst war es, die ihre Legende pflegte und ihre Person dahinter verbarg.

Hier ein Beispiel: Elisabeth ließ sich nur fotografieren, als sie sich auf der Höhe ihrer Schönheit fühlte — und wirklich auch war: in den sechziger Jahren. Diese Fotos bringen uns die etwa dreißigjährige Kaiserin Elisabeth ziemlich nahe: eine unerhört selbstbewußte, auch nach heutigen Maßstäben wunderschöne Frau, meist melancholisch, manchmal ironisch in die Kamera blickend, mit dem Flair einer zarten Märchenfee (S. 60—83).

Aus den späteren Jahren sind keine Fotos der Kaiserin bekannt. Denn in dem Augenblick, als sie trotz immenser Anstrengungen (lebenslanger Hungerkuren, intensiver sportlicher Aktivität, dreistündiger täglicher Haarpflege) ihre Schönheit schwinden sah, weigerte sie sich strikt, sich fotografieren zu lassen. Ab nun versteckte sie sich hinter der Legende einer wunderschönen Frau, die sie einmal gewesen war — im wörtlichen Sinn: Sie trat immer seltener in der Öffentlichkeit auf — und wenn, verbarg sie ihr Gesicht hinter dem schon sprichwörtlich gewordenen schwarzen Lederfächer, dem weißen Sonnenschirm oder ihren mannigfachen Gesichtsschleiern (S. 142/143).

Sie entzog sich den Blicken der Öffentlichkeit. Ihre Schüchternheit steigerte sich mit den Jahren zu einer Angst vor Menschen. Sie war unfähig, Kontakt aufzunehmen, ja eine harmlose Konversation zu führen. Sie weigerte sich, Persönliches preiszugeben und wirkte deshalb bei ihren Repräsentationspflichten wie eine Puppe, wie eine Schauspielerin ihrer selbst — ein Eindruck, der durch ihre konsequente öffentliche Schweigsamkeit unterstrichen und auch von ihr selbst bestätigt wurde: „Oft komme ich mir vor, wie dicht verschleiert, ohne es zu sein, wie in einer innerlichen Maskerade, im Costüm einer Kaiserin." Und heimlich dichtete die „holde" Kaiserin Verse wie diese:

Ich wollt', die Leute liessen mich
In Ruh' und ungeschoren,
Ich bin ja doch nur sicherlich
Ein Mensch, wie sie geboren.

Es tritt die Galle mir fast aus,
Wenn sie mich so fixieren;
Ich kröch' gern in ein Schneckenhaus
Und könnt' vor Wut krepieren.

Gewahr' ich gar ein Opernglas
Tückisch auf mich gerichtet,
Am liebsten sähe ich gleich das
Samt der Person vernichtet.

Zu toll wird endlich mir der Spass;
Und nichts mehr soll mich hindern;
Ich drehe eine lange Nas'
Und zeig ihnen den H…n'

Niemand außer der engsten Familie kannte das Gesicht der älteren Elisabeth. Die Maler und Zeitungsillustratoren machten sich ihr eigenes, von der Legende genährtes Bild von ihr. Denn sie konnten Elisabeth ja nicht so darstellen, wie sie sie zu sehen bekamen (wenn überhaupt): verschleiert, versteckt hinter dem Fächer und dem Sonnenschirm. Die Fotografen retuschierten nach und nach die einzig verfügbaren Fotos der jungen Sisi, um sie als Konterfeis der Vierzig-, Fünfzigjährigen glaubhafter zu machen.

Auch die großen gemalten Porträts haben nur beschränkten Aussagewert. Denn nur den wenigsten ihrer Maler stand Elisabeth Modell: in ihrer Brautzeit den Malern Piloty (S. 130) und Schrotzberg (S. 16 und 58), später nur noch dem französischen Hofmaler Franz Xaver Winterhalter, der 1864 die drei berühmtesten Sisi-Porträts schuf (S. 52—55).

Dem Maler Georg Raab, der die Kaiserin einige Male malte (S. 91 und 121) wurde immerhin gestattet, sich eine Zeitlang in den Vorräumen zu den Appartements der Kaiserin aufzuhalten. Hier durfte er sie sehen, wenn sie zufällig vorbeikam. Er mußte ganz rasch — und unbemerkt von der hohen Frau — seine Skizzen machen. Sie wollte nicht aufgehalten, nicht angestarrt werden und machte dem Maler die Aufgabe nicht leicht. Nicht von ungefähr hat das berühmte Elisabeth-Porträt von Raab aus dem Jahr 1867, das sie im ungarischen Krönungskleid zeigt (S. 93) Ähnlichkeit mit den Fotos, die am Krönungstag im Atelier gemacht wurden (S. 96/97).

Den Bildhauern ging es nicht anders. Und die vielen Statuetten und Plastiken, die es von Elisabeth gibt, geben keinen Aufschluß über ihre wahre Erscheinung. Auch Bitterlich, der Schöpfer des Elisabeth-Denkmals im Wiener Volksgarten, kannte die Kaiserin nicht aus eigener Anschauung. Er machte die Büste ebenfalls nach Porträts und Fotos Elisabeths, somit die Legende fortschreibend bis heute.

Die Diskrepanz zwischen dem Bild, das die Künstler und die Historiker von der Kaiserin Elisabeth machen, ist ungewöhnlich groß und reizvoll — was anhand der Biographie (Brigitte Hamann, Elisabeth, Kaiserin wider Willen, Amalthea-Verlag Wien 1982) leicht nachzuprüfen ist. Doch verliert Elisabeth in der Realität der historischen Quellen (vor allem ihrer erst seit kurzem bekannten eigenen Aussagen) keineswegs an Faszination. Gerade ihre Widersprüchlichkeit macht sie, die Kunstfigur wie die reale Person des Wiener Fin de siècle, für uns so anziehend.

Brigitte Hamann

Editorial

When we've looked at the almost three hundred pictures of Empress Elisabeth in this book, how much closer do we come to the real person? Can we really get a picture of her?

In order to bring about no false hopes the answer immediately is 'no'. The personality of the Empress is apparent in her letters and poems but certainly not in the artists' portraits and impressions. These only portray the 'Sisi'-legend of her that the people then saw, and wanted to see. The interesting, exciting and unpredictable woman 'Elisabeth' remains hidden.

The artists are in fact completely innocent in this matter. It was the Empress herself who cared for this legend and chose to hide behind it.

For example — she only allowed herself to be photographed when she felt at her best and this was in the sixties. Therefore we have a picture of a thirty year old, self-assured Empress who was extremely beautiful — even according to todays terms. At the same time we see her looking a trifle sad, and she even had a slightly ironic expression as she looked into the camera with this flair of a fragile fairy (s. pages 60—83).

There are no known photos from the later years; as soon as the moment came, despite great efforts on her part (starvation diets, lots of sport and three hourly hairs sessions) when she saw that her beauty was vanishing, she refused to be photographed. From that moment on she hid herself behind this legend of the beautiful woman that she once was. She took less part in public life and when obliged to she hid her face behind a black leather fan or a white parasol or one of the many veils which became associated with her (s. pages 142/143).

Her shyness developed to a real fear of people. She became incapable of making contact with people and of even holding the simplest of conversations. She refused to reveal anything concerning herself and so at official occasions gave the impression of being a show figure, a puppet; this impression became stronger due to her continued silence when in public. She herself made the following statement which proves these observations: "I often appear to myself as though I'm almost completely veiled and above all this I'm just wearing the costume of an Empress." And then secretly the 'faire' empress wrote poems which contained her anxieties, her thoughts, and displayed her extreme dread of people who stared at her.

Nobody outside the closest members of the family could observe the face of the ageing Elisabeth. Artists and illustrators made their own 'legend'-like pictures of her but they could not present her as she had become behind her fans, veils and sunshades. The photographers depended more and more on the old available photos of the young Sisi in order to make their portraits of the forty to fifty year old woman more acceptable.

Even the really big portraits have a limited value, for very few painters actually had Elisabeth as a model. In her early days as a bride she modelled for Piloty (page 130) and Schrotzberg (pages 16 and 58). Later she modelled for the famous French court artist Franz Xaver Winterhalter who in 1864 produced the three most well known Sisi portraits (pages 52—55).

Georg Raab who painted the Empress several times (pages 93 and 121) was permitted to stay in the proximity of her private rooms and here was allowed to glimpse at her if she by chance passed by. Then he quickly and in a discreet fashion had to make sketches of Her Majesty. She did not wish to be stopped, disturbed or stared at, so his task was made quite difficult. It wasn't by chance that the famous Elisabeth portrait by Raab in 1867, showing her in the Hungarian Coronation robes (page 93) displays such similarity with the photos taken on Coronation Day (pages 96/97) in the artist's studio.

The fate of the sculptors was not so different. The many statues and sculptures which exist of Elisabeth give very little information about the real looks of the Empress. Even Bitterlich, who is responsible for the Elisabeth statue in the Vienna Volksgarten didn't actually know the Empress personally. He made the bust according to portraits and photos of Elisabeth — thus prolonging the legend up to the present time.

The discrepancy between the picture which artists and historians make of Elisabeth is unusually great and stimulating (as can be seen in the biography 'Empress against her will' by Brigitte Hamann — Amalthea Verlag 1982). However in this historical research the Empress looses none of her fascination. It is this artificial object on the one hand and on the other hand this real personality of the Viennese 'Fin de siècle' which makes her so very appealing to us.

Brigitte Hamann

Ein Kind in Bayern
A Child in Bavaria

Elisabeth Amalie Eugenie, Herzogin in Bayern, wurde am Heiligabend 1837 in München geboren. Sie war das dritte von acht Kindern, und ihre Familie war mit weltlichen Gütern nicht übermäßig gesegnet. Das ist wohl auch der Grund, warum es so wenige Bilder des Kindes Elisabeth gibt.

Elisabeth Amalie Eugenie, Duchess in the kingdom of Bavaria, was born on Christmas Eve 1837 in Munich. She was the third of eight children and her family was not over-blessed with worldly possessions. This is probably the reason why there are so few portraits of Elisabeth as a child.

Herzogin Ludovika in Bayern mit ihren ältesten drei Kindern, Ludwig, Helene und der neugeborenen Sisi.

Duchess Ludovika with her three eldest children — Ludwig, Helene and the new born 'Sisi'.

Sisis Geburtshaus, das Palais Max auf der Ludwigstraße in München.

The Palais Max in Ludwig street, Munich where Sisi was born.

Zwei Kinderbilder als Zeugnis einer unbeschwerten, glücklichen Kindheit.

Two portraits as proof of a carefree and happy childhood.

Die Zehnjährige.

The ten year old Sisi.

Ländliche Kinderidylle am Starnberger See:
Sisi mit Carl Theodor.

Idyllic scenes from the country at Lake Starnberg:
Sisi with Carl Theodor.

Sisi mit ihrem Lieblingsbruder
Carl Theodor („Gackel").

Sisi with her favorite brother
Carl Theodor nicknamed 'Gackel'.

Das bescheidene, aber sehr idyllische Sommerschlößchen der Herzogsfamilie:
Possenhofen am Starnberger See.

The modest, but very idyllic summer castle of the Duke's family at Possenhofen on Lake Starnberg.

*Anton Fernkorn schuf diese Holzbüste
der zehnjährigen Sisi.*

*This wooden bust of the ten year old Sisi
was carved by Anton Fernkorn.*

Die Braut

The Bride

Die Kaiserbraut vor der Kulisse Ischls.

The Emperor's bride with Ischl in the background.

Die Verlobung Kaiser Franz Josephs mit der in Wien völlig unbekannten fünfzehnjährigen Sisi im August 1853 in Ischl war eine Sensation. Jedermann wollte wissen, wie die Kaiserbraut aussah: Porträtmaler und Kupferstecher hatten Hochkonjunktur.

The engagement of Emperor Franz Joseph with the 15 year old Sisi who was completely unknown in Vienna was a sensation at the time it was made public in Ischl in 1853. Everyone wanted to know what the Emperor's bride looked like. Painters and engravers were in great demand.

Erste Ausfahrt des Brautpaares mit dem Sechsspänner in Ischl.

The couple take their first coach outing in Ischl.

Rechte Seite:
Porträt im Verlobungsjahr von F. Hanfstaengl. Den Rosenkranz brachte der Kaiser seiner jungen Braut mitten im Winter als Geschenk bei einem seiner Münchenbesuche mit.

Right page:
A portrait in the year of the engagement by F. Hanfstaengl. The Emperor himself presented the roses to his young bride after a visit to Munich in the middle of winter.

Links: Eines von mehreren Sisi-Porträts von Franz Schrotzberg, heute aufbewahrt im Stift Göttweig.

Left — one of several portraits of Sisi by Franz Schrotzberg kept now in the monastery of Göttweig.

Sisi nimmt von ihrem geliebten Starnberger See Abschied: eine Phantasiezeichnung aus späteren Jahren.

Sisi takes leave of her beloved Lake Starnberg — a romantic drawing done in later years.

Auch diese Familienszene entsprang der Phantasie des Künstlers: das Kaiserpaar in Tracht auf dem Starnberger See. Herzog Max in Bayern auf seiner geliebten Zither spielend. Im Hintergrund die Sommerresidenz der herzoglichen Familie, Schloß Possenhofen.

This is also a picture from the artist's imagination — the Emperor and Empress in national costume on Lake Starnberg, with Duke Max of Bavaria playing his much loved zither. In the background is the summer reside of the duke's family — Possenhofen Castle.

Die Abfahrt der hohen Braut aus dem elterlichen Hause durch das Siegesthor.
München am 20. April 1854.

*The departure of the noble bride from her parent's house through the victory gate.
Munich, 20. April 1854.*

The reception of the Duchess Elisabeth in Nußdorf near Vienna on April 22, 1854.

Feierlicher Einzug der Kaiserbraut in der Haupt- und Residenzstadt am Tag vor der Trauung.

Ceremonial entry of the Emperor's bride in Vienna on the day before their wedding.

Hochzeit in Wien

The Marriage in Vienna

Am 24. April 1854 wurde das Kaiserpaar in der Augustinerkirche in Wien getraut. Eine Woche lang folgte ein Fest dem anderen.

On April 24th 1854 the wedding of the Emperor and his bride took place in the church of St. Augustine in Vienna. The festivities went on for a week.

Vertreter aller Stände huldigen dem Kaiserpaar nach der Hochzeit.
People from all stands of life congratulate the royal couple.

Modezeichnung vom Brautkleid.

The design of the bride's dress.

Festbeleuchtung in Wien, hier der Platz an der Freyung und der Prater.

Ceremonial illumination in Vienna. The scene here shows the Freyung Square and the Prater.

FRANZ JOSEF Kaiser von Österreich und Allerhöchst Dessen Frau ELISABETH Kaiserin von Oesterreich.

Trauung in der Augustinerkirche am 24. April.

The wedding in the church of St. Augustin on the April, 24.

Eintritts-Karte
in die erste Antekammer
zum Zusehen bei dem allerhöchsten Brautzuge
am 24. April 1854.

Nur giltig für

Der Einlaß beginnt um vier Uhr nachmittags und wird um sechs Uhr gänzlich geschlossen.

Die Herren erscheinen in Uniform; wer damit nicht versehen ist, im schwarzen Frack, mit weißer Cravate — die Frauen in gewählter Kleidung, ohne Hüte.

Die Zufahrt ist an der Bothschafterstiege im Schweizerhofe, wohin man nach der für diesen Tag bestimmten Fahrordnung gelangt.

Die neue Kaiserin wird dem Hofstaat vorgestellt.

The new Empress is presented at court.

Sisi im Brautschleier.

Sisi in her bridal veil.

Das Kaiserpaar am Hochzeitsabend bei der Beleuchtung der Stadt Wien am Kohlmarkt.

The Emperor and Empress at Kohlmarkt on the occasion of the illumination of Vienna on the evening of their wedding.

Linke Seite: Franz Joseph zeigt seiner jungen Frau die kaiserliche Haupt- und Residenzstadt Wien: rechts hinten der Stephansdom, links Kahlenberg und Leopoldsberg, davor die kaiserliche Sommerresidenz, Schloß Schönbrunn.

Left page: Franz Joseph presents the Imperial residence and residential town of Vienna to his young wife. In the background right one sees St. Stephens Cathedral, on the left the hills of Kahlenberg and Leopoldsberg, and in the foreground the Emperor's summer residence Schönbrunn Castle.

Das junge Kaiserpaar auf einer Porzellanmalerei ...
The young couple as painted on porcelain ...

... und in der offenen Kutsche, gemalt von A. Bensa.
... and in an open coach, painted by A. Bensa.

WAPPEN SEINER MAJESTÄT DES KAISERS.

WAPPEN IHRER MAJESTÄT DER KAISERIN.

The coat of arms of the Emperor (above) and of the Empress (below).

Nach den anstrengenden Hochzeitsfeiern erholte sich das junge Paar in den Flitterwochen in Schloß Laxenburg (im Hintergrund).

After a tiring wedding celebration the young couple relax on honeymoon at Laxenburg Castle (in the background).

Doppelporträt von Eduard Kaiser.

A double portrait by Eduard Kaiser.

Franz Joseph und Elisabeth als Gäste in der Kaiserloge des Hofburgtheaters.

Franz Joseph and Elisabeth as guests in the Emperor's box at the Hofburg theatre.

Das Brautpaar in Wiener Porzellan.

The wedding couple depicted in Viennese porcelain.

Die junge Mutter
The Young Mother

Das Kaiserpaar hatte vier Kinder: Sophie (geboren 1855, gestorben 1858), Gisela (geboren 1856), Rudolf (geboren 1858) und Marie Valerie (1868). Die Erziehung der ersten drei Kinder behielt sich Sisis Schwiegermutter vor, wodurch es zu erbitterten Familienkämpfen kam. Erst ihre „Einzige", Marie Valerie, ihr Lieblingskind, ließ sich Sisi nicht mehr entfremden.

The Imperial couple had four children: Sophie (born in 1855, who died in 1858), Gisela (born in 1856), Rudolf (born in 1858) and Marie Valerie (born in 1868). Sisi's mother in law maintained the right of bringing up the first three children and accordingly there were many bitter family quarrels. Sisi didn't allow her favourite child Marie Valerie, whom she called her 'only one One' to be taken out of her hands.

Porzellangruppe des Kaiserpaares mit dem ersten Kind.

The Imperial couple with their first child depicted in porcelain.

Die Kaiserfamilie 1857. Von links: Erzherzogin Sophie mit der kleinen Gisela, Erzherzog Franz Carl, Sisi, Franz Joseph mit Sophie.

The Imperial family in 1857. From the left: Archduchess Sophie with the small Gisela, Archduke Franz Carl, Sisi, Franz Joseph with Sophie.

Patriotisches Huldigungsbild zur Geburt der kleinen Sophie, 1855. Lithographie von Eduard Kaiser.

A picture in the style of patriotic admiration at the birth of Sophie in 1855. Lithography by Eduard Kaiser.

Elisabeth mit ihrer Schwiegermutter Sophie und den Kindern Gisela und Rudolf 1859 kurz vor ihrer Flucht nach Madeira.

Elisabeth and her mother in law Sophie and the children Gisela and Rudolf in 1859 shortly before her flight to Madeira.

*Aquarell von Josef Kriehuber: Sisi mit Gisela und dem neugeborenen Kronprinzen.
An der Wand eine Erinnerung an die erstgeborene, inzwischen gestorbene kleine Sophie.*

*A water painting by Joseph Kriehuber: Sisi with Gisela and the newly born Crown Prince.
On the wall a reminder of the first born child Sophie who had already died.*

Die junge Kaiserfamilie vor dem Bild des großen Urahns, Rudolf von Habsburg, nach dem der kleine Kronprinz seinen Namen erhielt. Die Wiege ist mit der österreichischen Kaiserkrone und dem Doppeladler verziert, das Kind trägt bereits den Orden des Goldenen Vlieses um den Hals: Ein großes Erbe soll getragen werden.

The young Imperial family in front of their great ancestor Rudolf von Habsburg, whose name was bestowed on the small Crown Prince. The cradle is decorated with the Imperial Crown of Austria and the double-headed eagle. The child is already wearing the order of the golden fleece. A great inheritance was to be continued.

Das Kaiserpaar mit den beiden ältesten Kindern, Sophie und Gisela.

The Imperial couple with the two eldest children Sophie and Gisela

Krankheit und Flucht
Illness and Escape

Nach sechsjähriger Ehe war das Glück des Kaiserpaares 1860 zu Ende. Die Kaiserin verließ nach schweren Differenzen ihre Familie, floh zuerst nach Possenhofen, dann nach Madeira und dann nach Korfu. Für die Öffentlichkeit gab man eine schwere Krankheit als Grund für die fast zweijährige Abwesenheit der jungen Kaiserin von Wien an.

After six years of marriage the happiness of the Emperor and Empress was at an end. Amidst grave differences the Empress left her family; first she fled to Possenhofen, then to Madeira and after that to Corfu. The reason given to the public for her absence from Vienna was a „severe illness".

Fotoserie des Wiener Fotografen Angerer von der kranken und sichtlich unglücklichen Elisabeth.

A series of pictures of the sick and apparently unhappy Elisabeth produced by the Viennese photographer Angerer.

Die einsame Villa auf Madeira, in der Sisi Zuflucht suchte.

The lonely villa on Madeira where Sisi sought refuge.

Sisi, auf Madeira Mandoline spielend, von ihren von ihren Hofdamen umgeben.

Sisi playing the mandoline in Madeira surrounded by her ladies in waiting.

Sisi, auf Madeira lustwandelnd.

Sisi having a leisurely walk in Madeira.

Die ganze Welt nahm Anteil an der Krankheit der jungen Kaiserin. Peter Rosegger war einer der vielen, die sich in die Einsamkeit und Traurigkeit Sisis hineinversetzten. Dieses Bild zeichnete er für den Volkskalender 1861

The whole world was interested in the young Empress's illness. The well known Austrian poet Peter Rosegger was one of the many people who tried to imagine what she was going through at this time. This picture he drew for the popular calendar of the year 1861.

Ihre beiden kleinen Kinder Gisela und Rudolf sah Elisabeth nach langer Trennung 1862 in Venedig wieder. Hier eine Gondelfahrt mit der Erzieherin des Kronprinzen, Charlotte Freifrau von Welden.

After a long period of separation Elisabeth saw her children Gisela and Rudolf in Venice. Here we see a trip on a gondola with Charlotte Freifrau von Welden who was the governess of the Crown Prince.

Sisi mit einer Hofdame in Venedig.

Sisi with a lady in waiting in Venice.

Viele Jahre lang absolvierte Sisi ihre Sommerkuren in Bad Kissingen. Hier traf sie mit anderen prominenten Gästen zusammen, so mit dem Zaren von Rußland und ihrem Vetter, dem jungen König Ludwig II. von Bayern.

For many years Sisi was a visitor at the baths in Kissingen. Here she met many prominent guests such as the Csar of Russia and her cousin, the young King Ludwig II. of Bavaria.

Portraits
Portraits

Die sechzehnjährige Kaiserin vor der Kulisse Wiens.

The sixteen year old Empress with Vienna as a background.

*Rechts:
Ein frühes Foto.*

*Right:
An early photograph.*

Kniestück von Josef Kriehuber 1863.

A three quarter length portrait by Josef Kriehuber taken in 1863.

Rechts: Zeichnung von Albert Decker.

Right: A picture drawn by Albert Decker.

*1864 kam der berühmte Hofmaler Franz Xaver Winterhalter (1805–1873) aus Paris nach Wien, um hier die Reichsten und Vornehmsten auftragsgemäß zu porträtieren – zu einem selbst für Wiener Hofverhältnisse horrenden Preis.
Von Kaiserin Elisabeth gibt es drei Bilder: das offizielle im Galakleid, mit den berühmten Diamantensternen im geflochtenen Haar (nebenstehend), und zwei private mit aufgelöstem Haar für den Kaiser, der beide in seinem Arbeitszimmer hängen hatte – bis über Sisis Tod hinaus (siehe folgende Doppelseite).*

*In 1864 the famous court painter Franz Xaver Winterhalter (1805–1873) came from Paris to Vienna to produce portraits of high society – at a price which was even horrifying to the Imperial household.
He made three pictures of Empress Elisabeth; the official one in state dress with the famous diamond stars and plaited hair (see opposite page) and two private ones where she poses with her hair hanging loosely over her shoulders. These were for the Emperor who had them both in his study – even after she died (see the following two pages).*

Diese Bilder hängen heute im Schloß Miramare bei Triest (links) und im Zisterzienserstift Lilienfeld (rechts).
These pictures are now to be seen in Castle Miramare near Triest (left) and in the Cistercian Monastery Lilienfeld (right).

Wohl das berühmteste Bild von Franz Schrotzberg. *Probably the most famous picture by Franz Schrotzberg.*

Lithographie von Adolf Douthage.   *Lithography by Adolf Douthage.*

Drei Bilder aus einer Fotoserie von Sisis Lieblingsfotografen Angerer in Wien um 1865.

Three pictures from a series by Sisi's favourite photographer Angerer, Vienna, about 1865.

In den sechziger Jahren engagierte Elisabeth die frühere Burg-theater-Coiffeuse Fanny Feifalik als Friseuse. Seit dieser Zeit trug sie die berühmtesten Flechtfrisuren ihres Jahrhunderts, die sie als „Steckbrieffrisuren" bezeichnete.

In the sixties Elisabeth hired the former official hair-dresser of the Burg-theatre, Fanny Feifalik. Since that time she wore the most famous plaited hairstyles of the century — which she referred to as a "warrant's-hairstyle".

Mitte der sechziger Jahre, auf dem Höhepunkt ihrer Schönheit, ließ sich Sisi oft und gern fotografieren, allerdings nicht mit ihren Kindern oder ihrem kaiserlichen Gatten, sondern am liebsten mit ihren Hunden oder allein (Fotos: Angerer, Wien).

In the middle of the sixties Sisi felt herself at the height of her beauty and allowed herself to be photographed frequently. However she did not want to be photographed with her children or her imperial husband but preferred to be shown with her dogs or on her own (Photo Angerer, Vienna).

Berühmte Fotoserie mit pelzverbrämtem Samtmantel und Hut, den Lieblingshund Shadow an der Seite, Mitte der sechziger Jahre.

A famous series of photos taken in the middle of the sixties showing the Empress in hat and velvet coat trimmed with ermine — at her side her favourite dog 'Shadow'.

Wieder mit Shadow im Atelier des Fotografen Angerer, Mitte der sechziger Jahre.

More photos with 'Shadow' taken in the studio of Angerer in the sixties.

Zwei wenig bekannte Fotos aus dem Fotoalbum von Sisis Enkelin, Gräfin Elisabeth Seefried.

Two less well known photos from Countess Elisabeth Seefried's collection — she was the granddaughter of the Empress.

Ganz, ganz selten sind Fotos, auf denen Sisi lächelt, wenn auch nur ein wenig, wie auf diesem. Fotoserie Mitte der sechziger Jahre von Albert, München.

Very rare are the photographs of a smiling Sisi — even if it happens to be just a faint smile as in this series of photos: These were produced in the Albert studio, Munich in the middle sixties.

Sisi im Reitkleid mit und ohne Pinscher (Foto Angerer).

Sisi in her riding habit with and without her fox-terrier.

Foto Angerer, Wien um 1865.
Photo Angerer about 1865.

Bisher ist kein einziges gemeinsames Atelierfoto des Kaiserpaares aufgetaucht. Mit ihrem Lieblingsbruder, Herzog Carl Theodor in Bayern, allerdings ließ sich Sisi fotografieren.

Fotos: Angerer, Wien

Up 'til this point no studio photo of the Emperor and Empress has come to light. However Sisi did allow photos of herself to be taken with her favourite brother Duke Carl Theodor of Bavaria.

Photo: Angerer, Vienna.

Fotos um 1860.

Photos about 1860.

Sisi mit ihrem Bruder Carl Theodor und dessen Frau, Marie José, geborene Prinzessin von Braganza.

Sisi with her brother Carl Theodor and his wife Marie José, in her own right Princess of Braganza.

Mit Shadow im Fotoatelier Angerer in Wien.

Studio photos from Angerer showing the Empress with her dog 'Shadow'.

Fotoserie Angerer aus den sechziger Jahren.

A series of photos taken by Angerer in the mid-sixties.

Foto aus dem Atelier Albert in München.

A photo from the Albert studio, Munich.

Spätes Foto von Angerer, Wien um 1870.

One of Angerer's late photos taken in Vienna around 1870.

Zwei Gemälde des ungarischen Malers Gyula Benczur Mitte der siebziger Jahre.

Two oil paintings by the Hungarian artist Gyula Benczur, produced in the mid-seventies.

Foto um 1870.

Photograph taken around 1870.

Königin von Ungarn
The Queen of Hungary

Wenn sich Sisi auch im allgemeinen aus der Politik heraushielt, so machte sie doch eine große Ausnahme, als es um Ungarn ging: Ihr Einfluß war 1867 entscheidend für die Schaffung des „Ausgleichs", der „Versöhnung" mit dem „Rebellenvolk" der Ungarn. Besiegelung dieser Versöhnung war die Königskrönung in Budapest. Elisabeth lernte fließend ungarisch sprechen und schreiben und hielt sich mehr und mehr nicht in Wien, sondern in Budapest auf — zum Ärger des Wiener Hofes.

Although Sisi usually kept herself well out of politics she made one great exceptions as far as Hungary was concerned. It was due to her influence that in 1867 the so called 'Ausgleich', the reconciliation with the supposedly rebellious people of Hungary was established. The official seal of this reconciliation was the crowning of the Emperor as King of Hungary in Budapest. Elisabeth learnt to speak and write Hungarian fluently and spent more and more time in Budapest — much to the anger of the court in Vienna.

Die ungarische Königsfamilie vor Schloß Gödöllö bei Budapest, das die ungarische Nation dem neuen Königspaar als Privatresidenz schenkte.

The King and Queen in front of the castle of Gödöllö near Budapest, which was presented to the new King and Queen by the Hungarian nation for their private use.

Sisi als Königin von Ungarn.

Sisi as Queen of Hungary.

Feierlicher Einzug Ihrer k.k. Majestäten des Kaisers u. Königs Franz Josef I. und Höchstdessen Gemahlin der Kaiserin u. Königin Elisabeth in die Hauptstadt Ungarns am 29. Janer 1866.

Feierlicher Einzug Franz Josephs und Elisabeths in Budapest im Januar 1866. Rechts die Elisabethbrücke, die die beiden Städte Ofen und Pest verbindet.

Ceremonial entry of Franz Joseph and Elisabeth into Budapest in January 1866. On the right we see the Elisabeth Bridge which combines the two parts of Budapest — Ofen and Pest.

Bürgerball in Pest 1866.

The citizen's ball in Pest, 1866.

Ankunft in Debrezin.
Arrival at Debrezin.

Franz Joseph und Elisabeth beim Volksfest in Gyula 1857…
Franz Joseph and Elisabeth at a fair in Gyula…

... *und beim Volksfest in Großwardein.*
... *and at a fair in Großwardein.*

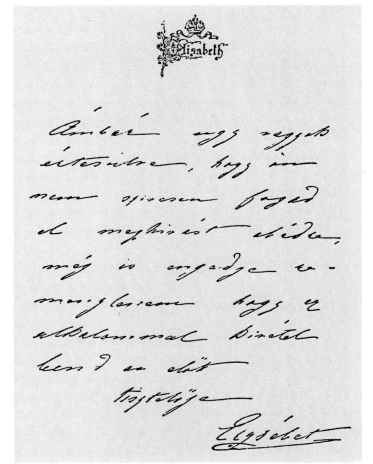

Schriftprobe aus einem ungarischen Text Elisabeths.
A specimen of Elisabeth's handwriting chosen from one of her works written in Hungarian.

Demonstrativ trug Sisi in den sechziger Jahren ungarische Magnatentracht.

In the sixties Sisi wore the dress of the Hungarian upper class as a demonstration of her affection for the Hungarian people.

Am 8. Juni 1867 wurden Franz Joseph und Elisabeth in der Mathiaskirche in Ofen gekrönt. Die heilige Stephanskrone wurde dem neuen König auf den Kopf gesetzt, der Königin aber nach altem Brauch über die rechte Schulter gehalten. Graf Gyula Andrássy assistierte dem Fürstprimas von Ungarn bei der Krönung.

On June 8th, 1867 Franz Joseph and Elisabeth were crowned in the Mathias Church in Ofen. St. Stephen's holy crown was placed on the new King's head but according to old custom held over the Queen's right shoulder. Earl Gyula Andrássy assisted at the crowning ceremony which was led by the Hungarian Primate.

Elisabeth fährt im feierlichen Zug zur Krönungskirche.

Elisabeth is driven in a ceremonial procession to the church where she will be crowned.

Die neue Königin von Ungarn, neben ihr auf dem Samtkissen die heilige Stephanskrone.

The new Queen of Hungary and next to her on a velvet cushion the Stephen's Crown, sacred symbol to the Hungarians.

Die Krönung der Königin.

The crowning of the Queen.

Folgende Seite:
Die Huldigung für das Königspaar von Ungarn nach der Krönung. Graf Gyula Andrássy (vorne rechts) bringt das „Eljen" aus, in das alle Anwesenden einfallen.

Bei den tagelangen Festlichkeiten nach der Krönung war stets Andrássy in der Nähe des Königspaares, und kein Illustrator vergaß die Verdienste dieses Politikers für den „Ausgleich" gebührend herauszustellen (hier im Vordergrund links, mit dem Sektglas ein Hoch auf das Königspaar ausrufend).

Next page:
Paying homage to the King and Queen of Hungary after the crowning ceremony. Earl Gyula Andrássy (front right) calls out the 'Eljen' which is joined in by all present.

Andrássy was always near the royal couple during the many days of celebrations and none of the illustrators forgot to stress the merits of this politician in connection with the 'Ausgleich'. In the second picture Andrássy is to be seen in the foreground left with his champagne glass which is raised in a toast for the royal couple.

Sisi im ungarischen Krönungskleid, gemalt von Georg Raab 1867.

Sisi in the Hungarian Coronation dress painted by Georg Raab, 1867.

Elisabeth 1876 an der Bahre Franz Deáks, des „Weisen der ungarischen Nation". Diese Szene wurde zu einer nationalen Legende Ungarns und inspirierte viele Maler und Illustratoren.

Elisabeth in 1876 at the coffin of Franz Deák — the 'sage of the Hungarian nation'. This scene became a national legend of Hungary and inspired many painters and illustrators.

Links: Kolorierte Lithographie nach Franz Ruß.

Left: A coloured lithography copying picture of Franz Ruß.

Fotoserie von der neuen Königin Ungarns am Krönungstag.
A series of photos of the new Queen of Hungary on Coronation Day.

Familienleben in Gödöllö: von links: Kronprinz Rudolf, Franz Joseph, Elisabeth mit der 1868 in Budapest geborenen Erzherzogin Marie Valerie, Erzherzogin Gisela.

Family life in Gödöllö. From the left: Crown Prince Rudolf, Franz Joseph, Elisabeth with Archduchess Marie Valerie, who was born in Budapest, in 1868, and Archduchess Gisela.

Sisi legte großen Wert auf eine rein ungarische Umgebung, wie auf diesem Bild. Von links: Franz Joseph mit Gyula Andrássy, die ungarische Amme mit der kleinen Marie Valerie, dahinter Elisabeths Vorleserin und enge Freundin Ida Ferenczy, Elisabeth, Gisela und Rudolf. Im Hintergrund rechts die Hofdame Gräfin Marie Festetics mit Sisis Obersthofmeister Baron Franz Nopsca.

Sisi placed great value on her Hungarian surroundings, as this picture clearly shows. From the left: Franz Joseph with Gyula Andrássy, the Hungarian nurse with the small Marie Valerie; behind: Elisabeth's close friend Ida Ferenczy who was also her reading companion. In the center: Elisabeth, Gisela and Rudolf. In the background right a lady in waiting, Countess Marie Festetics with Sisi's Lord High Steward Baron Franz Nopcsa.

Repräsentation
Representation

Das junge Kaiserpaar betend beim Marienfest Am Hof am 22. Juli 1855 in Wien, damit die enge Verbundenheit zwischen Thron und Altar demonstrierend. Einen Monat später wurde das Konkordat geschlossen.

The young Emperor and Empress at prayer on the day of the Holy Mary festival on July 22nd, 1855 in Vienna, Am Hof. This was an occasion to demonstrate the close relationship between the throne and the church. One month later the Concordat-treaty between the Vatican and Vienna was signed.

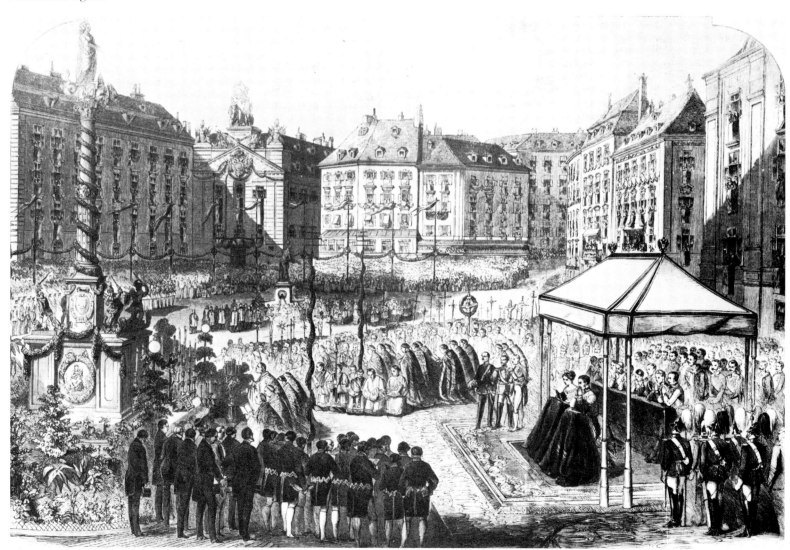

Aus Dankbarkeit, daß Kaiser Franz Joseph das Attentat 1853 überlebt hatte, wurde die Votivkirche in Wien gestiftet. Im Vordergrund links die Eltern des Kaisers, Erzherzogin Sophie und Erzherzog Franz Carl, mit dem jüngsten Bruder des Kaisers, Erzherzog Ludwig Viktor. Die schwangere Kaiserin steht hinter ihrem Gatten, der den Grundstein legt.

The Votiv Church in Vienna was founded and built to show Franz Joseph's gratefulness after he survived an attempt on his life. In the foreground left are the Emperor's parents, Archduchess Sophie and Archduke Franz Carl and the Emperor's youngest brother Archduke Ludwig Victor. The pregnant Empress stands behind her husband who is laying the foundation stone.

Franz Joseph und der Fürsterzbischof von Prag, Kardinal Friedrich Schwarzenberg mit der Kaiserin bei der Grundsteinlegung der Kirche in Prag-Karolinental 1854.

Franz Joseph and the Archbishop of Prague Cardinal Friedrich Schwarzenberg with the Empress at the occasion of laying the foundation stone of the church in Prague's Karolinental in 1854.

Zur Demonstration der österreichischen Herrschaft in der Lombardei und Venetien verbrachte das Kaiserpaar im Winter 1856/57 einige Monate in Oberitalien.

In the winter of 1856 and 1857 the Emperor and Empress spent a few months in the north of Italy to demonstrate the Austrian rule over Lombardy and Venetia.

Empfang des kaiserlichen Schiffes in Venedig.

Reception of the Imperial boat in Venice.

Das Kaiserpaar beim Verlassen des Marcusdomes in Venedig …

The Emperor and Empress leaving St. Marcus …

... und in der
Mailänder Oper.

... and in the
Opera of Milan.

Feierlicher Empfang im Hafen von Triest.

Ceremonial reception in Triest harbour.

Stadtbeleuchtung in Padua aus Anlaß des Kaiserbesuches.

Illumination of the town of Padua in honour of the visit by the Emperor.

Die Begeisterung der Italiener für das österreichische Kaiserpaar hielt sich in Grenzen. Die wenigen winkenden Menschen am Straßenrand waren entweder Österreicher oder wurden für ihr Winken bezahlt.

The enthusiasm of the Italians for the Emperor and Empress was more than limited. The few people waving on the streets were either Austrians or people paid for their patriotism.

Sisi besucht in Verona ein „Negererziehungsinstitut", wo arme afrikanische Waisenkinder zu Missionaren ausgebildet wurden.

Sisi visits an educational institute for negroes in Verona where poor African orphans were trained as missionaries.

Elisabeth empfängt in der Burg von Ofen ungarische Magnatenfrauen.

Elisabeth receives ladies of the Hungarian ruling class in the castle at Ofen.

Elisabeth bei der Schlußsteinfeier des Elisabethiniums in Budapest.

Elisabeth laying the finishing stone at the Elisabethinium in Budapest.

Politischer Gipfel in Salzburg 1867: Treffen des österreichischen und französischen Kaiserpaares. Im Vordergrund rechts Elisabeth, links Eugénie (im schockierend kurzen Rock).

A political top level meeting in Salzburg in 1867 between the Austrian and French Imperial couples. In the foreground right Elisabeth, left Eugénie (in a shockingly short dress).

Rechts: Spalier für das Königspaar.

On the right a lane of honour is formed for the royal couple.

Die Kaiserfamilie mit den berühmtesten Gästen der Weltausstellung in der Rotunde, dem Ort der Ausstellung. Rechts sitzend der Schah von Persien, hinter ihm der russische Außenminister Graf Gortschakow, der deutsche Kronprinz, Fürst Bismarck und Graf Andrássy, der zu dieser Zeit Außenminister von Österreich-Ungarn war. Zwischen Kaiser Franz Joseph und Kronprinz Rudolf der deutsche Kaiser Wilhelm I.

The Imperial family with the most famous guests of the World Fair in the Vienna 'Rotunde'. Right, seated is the Shah of Persiah, behind him to the right the Russian foreign minister Count Gortschakow, the German Crown Prince, Count Bismarck and Earl Andrássy, who was then foreign minister of Austro-Hungary. The German Emperor Wilhelm I. stands between Franz Joseph and Crown Prince Rudolf.

Die Eröffnung der Weltausstellung im Jahre 1873.

Ehrengäste bei der Eröffnung waren das deutsche Kronprinzenpaar (der spätere Kaiser Friedrich III., auf dem Podium ganz rechts, Kronprinzessin Viktoria rechts neben Elisabeth sitzend).

Honorary guests at the opening ceremony were the German Crown Prince and Princess (the later Emperor Frederik III. standing at the very right of the podium, Crown Princess Victoria sits to the right of Elisabeth).

1873 war Wien Schauplatz der Weltausstellung in der eigens für diesen Anlaß gebauten Rotunde im Prater. Die Mitglieder der Kaiserfamilie waren wochenlang mit festlichen Empfängen und Diners für die Gäste aus aller Welt ausgelastet.

In 1873 Vienna was the stage for the World Fair in the so called 'Rotunde' which was specially built for this occasion in the Prater. The members of the Imperial family were fully occupied for weeks entertaining guests from all over the world.

Auch die erst vor vier Jahren eröffnete neue Oper am Ring war eine Attraktion für die Ausstellungsgäste. Das Kaiserpaar mit dem deutschen Kronprinzen in der Hofloge.

A special attraction was also the new Opera (on the Ring Road) which had been opened only four years previously. The picture shows the Emperor and Empress with the German Crown Prince entering the royal box.

Kaiserin Augusta, die Gemahlin Wilhelms I., zwischen dem Kaiserpaar in der Hofloge der kaiserlichen Hofoper, rechts Erzherzog Arbrecht.

Empress Augusta, wife of Wilhelm I. seated between the Emperor and Empress in the royal box — on the right is the Archduke Albrecht.

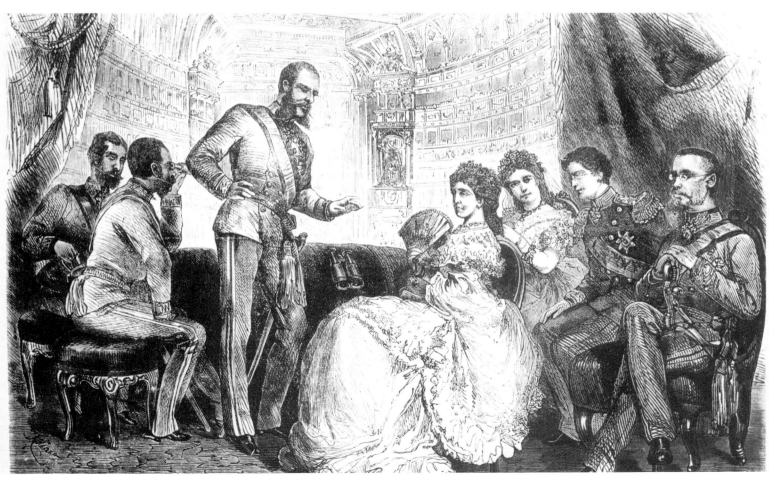

Die Kaiserin auf der Ringstrasse.

Elisabeth ließ sich in den siebziger Jahren immer seltener in Wien sehen und flüchtete selbst vor patriotischen Kundgebungen. Als sie im Dezember 1873 bei einem Spaziergang auf der Ringstraße erkannt wurde, flüchtete sie mit einem herbeigerufenen Fiaker. Im Wagen die jüngste Tochter Marie Valerie.

In the seventies Elisabeth was seen less and less in the public and escaped if possible even from patriotic demonstrations. When she was recognized taking a walk on the Ring Road in December 1873 she fled with a carriage ('Fiaker') which she beckoned quickly. In the carriage sits her youngest daughter Marie Valerie.

Beleuchtung der Haupt- und Residenzstadt Wien aus Anlaß des 25jährigen Regierungsjubiläums Franz Josephs im Dezember 1873. Kaiser und Kronprinz nehmen die Huldigungen auf der Ringstraße im offenen Wagen entgegen. Sisi fährt in einem geschlossenen Wagen, das Gesicht tief verschleiert und dadurch unkenntlich gemacht, hinter ihnen.

The illumination of the Imperial and residential town of Vienna in December 1873 on the occasion of the 25th Jubilee of Franz Joseph's reign. Emperor and Crown Prince respond to the homage along the Ring Road as they travel in an open carriage. Sisi sits in a closed carriage, her face almost completely veiled and thus made unrecognizable.

Die Salzburger Kuraufenthalte Kaiser Wilhelms I. wurden zu politischen Gesprächen und zur Anbahnung der deutsch-österreichischen Freundschaft genützt.

When Emperor Wilhelm I. stayed at the baths in Salzburg the opportunity was used for political talks and for paving the way for a German-Austrian friendship.

Einige Winter verbrachte Elisabeth im milden Klima Merans, wo sie auch der Kaiser besuchte. Hier mit Kronprinz Rudolf beim Schützenfest in Meran im April.

Elisabeth resided for several winters in the mild climate of Meran where the Emperor visited her. Here they can be seen with Crown Prince Rudolf at an Alpine shooting match in Meran in April 1871.

Elisabeth nimmt mit der deutschen Kaiserin Augusta, die Cour beim Fest des Grafen Andrássy 1873 ab. Neben ihnen stehen rechts Erzherzog Albrecht, Kaiser Franz Joseph und Gyula Andrássy.

Elisabeth and the German Empress Augusta officially receive the guests at a celebration given by Earl Andrássy in 1873. Beside them we see Archduke Albrecht, Emperor Franz Joseph and Gyula Andrássy.

Elisabeth 1888 beim Hofkonzert zwischen ihrem Sohn Rudolf und dessen Erzfeind Kaiser Wilhelm II. sitzend.

Elisabeth at a court concert in 1888 seated between her son Rudolf and his arch-enemy Emperor Wilhelm II.

Galadiner zu Ehren Kaiser Wilhelms II. in der Hofburg im Oktober 1888.

A state dinner in honour of Emperor Wilhelm II. in the Hofburg in Oct. 1888.

Elisabeth im berühmten Rubin-Schmuck.
Elisabeth in the famous ruby-jewellery.

◄
Die Kaiserin beim Hofball 1886 in Wien neben ihrer Schwiegertochter Stefanie. In Bildmitte Kronprinz Rudolf.

The Empress at the Imperial Ball in 1886 in Vienna. Beside her is her daughter-in-law Stephanie. In the middle Crown Prince Rudolf.

Elisabeth und Franz Joseph zu Besuch in Schloß Miramare bei Erzherzog Maximilian (rechts vorne) und Charlotte, dem späteren Kaiserpaar von Mexiko.

Elisabeth and Franz Joseph visiting Archduke Maximilian (foreground right) and Charlotte, the later Emperor and Empress of Mexico at Miramare Castle.

Das Kaiserpaar bei der feierlichen Enthüllung des Maria-Theresien-Denkmals in Wien im Mai 1888.

The Emperor and Empress at the official unveiling ceremony of the Maria-Theresia statue in Vienna in May 1888.

Die Kaiserbegegnung von Kremsier 1885 sollte die Zwistigkeiten zwischen Österreich-Ungarn und Rußland in der Balkanpolitik beilegen. Das Kaiserpaar empfängt das Zarenpaar am Bahnhof von Kremsier.

The meeting of Emperors at Kremsier 1885 was supposed to end political differences between Austro-Hungary and Russia concerning the Balkans. The Emperor and Empress receive the Csar and his wife at Kremsier railway station.

Trösterin der Armen
Comforter of the Poor

Kaiserlicher Besuch im Allgemeinen Krankenhaus Wien.
Imperial visit to the General Hospital in Vienna.

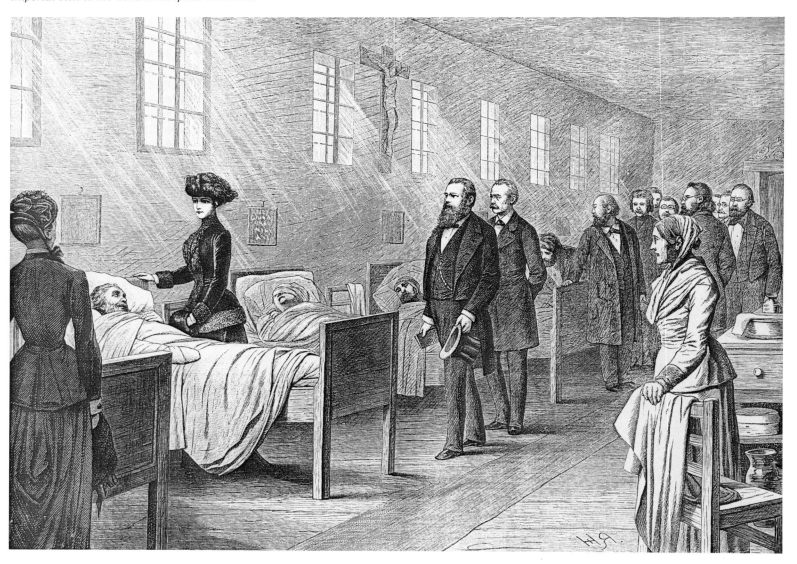

Das Volk aller Nationen erhoffte sich ein mildtätiges Herrscherpaar.

People of all nations hoped for a benevolent Imperial couple.

Elisabeth besucht mit Fürstin Marie zu Hohenlohe-Schillingsfürst eine Volksküche im 2. Wiener Bezirk.

Elisabeth and Countess Marie zu Hohenlohe-Schillingsfürst visit a Salvation army type institution called 'Volksküche' (people's kitchen) in the second district of Vienna.

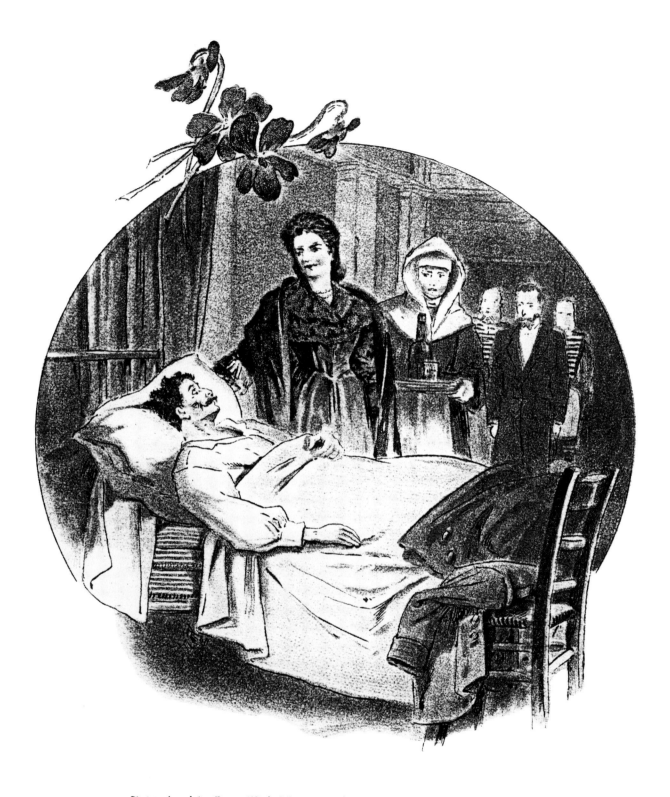

„Jetzt, da ich Eure Majestät an meinem Bette gesehen, habe ich keinen Wunsch mehr –"

„… now that I have seen Your Majesty at my bed I have no more wishes …"

Das interessante Blatt

Nr. 45. — Wien, 11. November 1886. — V. Jahrg.

Der Besuch der Kaiserin in der Irrenanstalt.

Kaiserin Elisabeth wohnt in der Frauenabtheilung der Irrenanstalt einer Hypnotisirung bei. (Siehe Seite 2.)

Die heutige Nummer ist 16 Seiten stark.

So wenig sich Elisabeth auch bei offiziellen Anlässen sehen ließ — Irrenhäuser besuchte sie, wann und wo immer es ging. Sie interessierte sich für neue Therapien bei Geisteskranken, so auch für die damals sensationelle Behandlung durch Hypnose.

As little as Elisabeth liked public appearances somehow she visited mental asylums wherever and whenever possible.
She was interested in new treatments for these patients and therefore also in hypnosis which was then the sensational idea of the day.

Ein sehr seltenes Schauspiel: die Kaiserin nimmt in demütig-frommer Haltung an der traditionellen Gründonnerstagszeremonie in Wien teil und wäscht zwölf ausgewählten armen alten Frauen die Füße. Rechts der Kaiser bei der Zeremonie.

A very rare spectacle — the Empress in a humble position taking part in the traditional ceremony of Maundy Thursday, washing the feet of twelve selected poor old women in Vienna. Right of her the Emperor performing the same ceremony.

Das Kaiserpaar besucht ein Altersheim.

The Imperial couple visit an old people's home.

So stellte sich das Volk seine Kaiserin-Königin vor: Als Mutter des Volkes Arme und Kranke tröstend (Elisabeth hier im ungarischen Krönungskleid). Plakette von Stefan Schwarz

This is how the people imagined the Empress-Queen as mother of the people, comforting the poor and sick. Elisabeth is seen here in her Hungarian Coronation dress — engraving by Stephan Schwarz.

Die Reiterin
The Equestrian

Schon als Kind war Sisi, ebenso wie ihre Geschwister, sehr sportlich. Ihre besondere Liebe galt dem Reiten. Daß sie ihr erstes Geld als Zirkusreiterin im Privatzirkus ihres Vaters Max verdiente, ist eine Legende. Doch gehörte Elisabeth zu den besten Reiterinnen ihrer Zeit. Sie war eine vorzügliche Jagd- und Dressurreiterin und feierte in den siebziger Jahren bei den englischen und irischen Parforcejagden Triumphe.

As a child Sisi and her brothers and sisters were very interested in all sports and her special love was for horses. Nevertheless it is only a legend that she earned her first pay as a circus rider in the private circus of her father Max. However Elisabeth was one of the best riders of her time. She was excellent at hunting and in the art of precise movement and had tremendous success in the English and Irish competitions during the seventies.

Das junge Kaiserpaar in Ischl zu Pferd. Hinter ihm der kaiserliche Generaladjutant Graf Grünne.

The young Emperor and Empress on horseback in Ischl — behind them the Emperor's Adjutant-General Count Grünne.

*Rechte Seite:
Dieses Porträt der fünfzehnjährigen Sisi vor ihrem Elternhaus Possenhofen war das Weihnachtsgeschenk für den jungen Bräutigam Kaiser Franz Joseph im Verlobungsjahr 1853. Der Maler war Piloty.*

*Right page:
This portrait of the fifteen year old Sisi depicting her with her parents' house Possenhofen as a background was a Christmas present for the young groom Franz Joseph in the year of their engagement 1853. It was painted by Piloty.*

Eduard Kaiser, Das junge Kaiserpaar zu Pferd im Lainzer Tiergarten.

The young Emperor and Empress on horseback in the Lainzer park — painted by Edward Kaiser.

Die ganz junge Sisi zu Pferd.   Wiener Biskuitporzellan.

The very young Sisi on horseback   (Viennese porcelain).

Rechts: Dieses Reiterbild schenkte die junge Kaiserin ihrem väterlichen Vertrauten Graf Grünne.

Right: This equestrian picture was given by the young Empress to her trustworthy friend Count Grünne.

Um sich als Reiterin körperlich leistungsfähig zu erhalten, absolvierte Elisabeth täglich ein ausgiebiges Gymnastik- und Turnprogramm. In jedem ihrer Wohnsitze — auch wie hier der Wiener Hofburg — ließ sie sich ein eigenes Turnzimmer einrichten.

In order to keep herself physically fit for riding Elisabeth kept to a strict and extensive fitness programme. In each of her homes — as here in the Hofburg at Vienna — she had her own gymnasium.

Sisi, selbst kutschierend, im Park von Laxenburg.

Sisi driving a carriage in Laxenburg Park.

Im Hof des Schlosses Gödöllö ließ sich die Kaiserin eine Manege bauen und arbeitete dort mit berühmten Zirkusreitern. Gemälde von Wilhelm Richter 1876.

Elisabeth had a circus ring built in the courtyard of Gödöllö castle and there worked with famous circus riders. Oil painting by Wilhelm Richter.

Fotoserie von Angerer, Wien um 1870.

A series of photographs by Angerer, Vienna around 1870.

Das Kaiserpaar auf der Reitjagd in Göding. Gemälde von Julius von Blaas. Um 1860.

The Emperor and Empress out hunting in Göding. Oil painting by Julius von Blaas about 1860.

*Rechte Seite:
Wilhelm Richter,
Die Kaiserin zu Pferd 1876,
Kohlezeichnung.*

Right page:
The Empress on horseback 1876 — a charcoal drawing by Wilhelm Richter.

Gemälde von Wilhelm Richter, um 1875.

Oil painting by Wilhelm Richter about 1975.

Elisabeth und ihr Pilot Bay Middleton setzen über eine Hecke. Im Vordergrund der englische Gastgeber Lord Harrington. (Zeichnung im Besitz des englischen Königshauses.)

Elisabeth and her horse pilot Bay Middleton jump over a hedge. In the foreground the English host Lord Harrington (drawing owned by the English Royal family).

Rechte Seite:
Ohne Unfälle ging es auch bei einer so guten Reiterin nicht ab: Im September 1883 gerät Sisis Pferd bei einem Ritt in der Nähe des „Toten Weibes" bei Mürzsteg in ein Brückenloch. Ein Jäger rettet die Kaiserin vor dem Absturz in die Tiefe.

Right page:
Even such an excellent rider as Elisabeth couldn't escape an accident. In September 1883 Sisi's horse broke through a bridge near Mürzsteg. A hunter saved the Empress from falling into the abyss.

Elisabeth im Park von Biberach bei Wiesbaden.

Elisabeth in the Biberach Park near Wiesbaden.

Elisabeth in Baden-Baden. Neben ihr auf den Ponies ihre jüngste Tochter Marie Valerie und ihre Nichte Gräfin Trani.

Elisabeth in Baden-Baden. On the ponies beside her we see her youngest daughter Marie Valerie and her niece Countess Trani.

Selbst beim Reiten hatte Elisabeth stets ihren Fächer bei sich, um ihr Gesicht vor Neugierigen und Fotografen zu verbergen.

Even whilst riding Elisabeth had her fan at hand to cover her face from curious onlookers and photographers.

Familienleben
Family Life

Das Kaiserpaar in den sechziger Jahren.
The Emperor and Empress in the sixties.

Sisi im Mittelpunkt einer großen Familie: links Sophie mit Rudolf, vorne Gisela, rechts Sisis Schwiegervater Franz Carl. Oben von links nach rechts: die vier Söhne der Erzherzogin Sophie: Ludwig Viktor, Kaiser Franz Joseph, Karl Ludwig (mit Maria Annunziata) und Max (mit Charlotte).

Sisi surrounded by her large family: left Sophie with Rudolf, in the front Gisela, right Sisi's father-in-law Franz Carl. Above from left to right: the four sons of Archduchess Sophie, Ludwig Viktor, Emperor Franz Joseph, Karl Ludwig (with Maria Annunziata) and Max (with Charlotte).

Die Kaiserfamilie nach Sisis Rückkehr aus Korfu 1862.

The Imperial family after Sisi's return from Corfu, 1862.

Die Kaiserfamilie um 1860: In der Mitte das Kaiserpaar, oben die ältesten beiden Kinder, Gisela und Rudolf, links und rechts oben die Eltern des Kaisers, Erzherzogin Sophie und Erzherzog Franz Carl, links und rechts unter dem Kaiserpaar der jüngere Bruder Franz Josephs, Erzherzog Ferdinand Max, mit seiner Gemahlin Charlotte (das spätere Kaiserpaar von Mexico), links und rechts unten der zweite Bruder Karl Ludwig mit seiner Gemahlin Maria Annunziata (die Eltern der Erzherzöge Franz Ferdinand und Otto), unten der jüngste Bruder Ludwig Viktor.

The Imperial family around 1860. In the middle are the Emperor and Empress. Above the eldest children Gisela and Rudolf. To the left and right above the Emperor's parents Archduchess Sophie and Archduke Franz Carl. Left and right below the royal couple are the younger brother of Franz Joseph, Archduke Ferdinand Max with his wife Charlotte (the later Emperor and Empress of Mexico). At the bottom left and right are the second brother Karl Ludwig and his wife Maria Annunziata (the parents of the Archdukes Franz Ferdinand and Otto) and at the very bottom the youngest brother Ludwig Viktor.

Rechts: Das Kaiserpaar mit dem ersten Kind, Sophie. Stehend die Eltern des Kaisers und seine drei jüngeren Brüder.

Right: The Imperial couple with the first child Sophie. We see the parents and the three younger brothers of the Emperor standing.

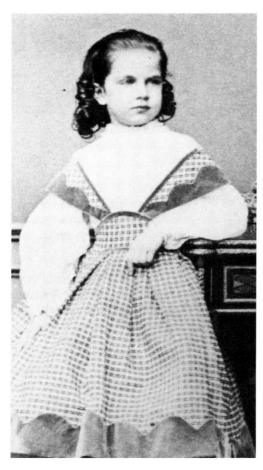

Die ältere Tochter Gisela (1856—1932) wuchs ohne mütterliche Liebe auf.

The eldest daughter Gisela (1856—1932) grew up without motherly affection.

Elisabeth war noch nicht 35 Jahre alt, als ihre Tochter Gisela sich 1873 mit 16 Jahren verlobte und heiratete. Hochzeit war wieder in der Augustinerkirche in Wien.

Elisabeth hadn't reached the age of 35 when her daughter Gisela was engaged and married in 1873 at the age of sixteen. The wedding took place again in the Augustine church in Vienna.

Eine Familienidylle, anläßlich Giselas Verlobung gemalt. Von links: der 15jährige Rudolf, Elisabeth, die fünfjährige Marie Valerie, das Brautpaar Gisela und Prinz Leopold von Bayern, Kaiser Franz Joseph.

An idyllic scene of the family painted on the occasion of Gisela's engagement. From the left: Rudolf, aged 15, Elisabeth, Marie Valerie, then five years old, the bride and groom, Gisela and Price Leopold of Bavaria, and Emperor Franz Joseph.

Kronprinz Rudolf — ein Kind in Uniform.

Crown Prince Rudolf — a child in uniform.

Eine seltene Darstellung: Elisabeth mit ihrem Sohn Rudolf, hier bei einer Schlittenfahrt in Ungarn, 1876 (von Theodor Breidwiser).

A rare picture of Elisabeth with her son Rudolf on a sledge excursion in Hungary, 1876 (by Theodor Breidwiser).

1881 wurde die Kaiserfamilie durch eine Schwiegertochter vergrößert: Rudolf heiratete Stephanie von Belgien. Verlobungsbild, von links: Franz Joseph, der Brautvater König Leopold I. der Belgier, Elisabeth, Stephanie und Rudolf, die Brautmutter Marie Henriette von Belgien, eine geborene Habsburgerin.

The Imperial family was enlarged by a daughter-in-law in 1881: Rudolf married Stefanie of Belgium. Engagement picture — from left: Franz Joseph, the brides' father King Leopold of the Belgians, Elisabeth, Stefanie and Rudolf, the brides' mother Marie Henriette of Belgium, herself a born Habsburg.

Die Kaiserin empfängt in Schönbrunn ihre neue Schwiegertochter. So innig wie auf dieser Illustration war das Verhältnis der beiden Frauen allerdings keineswegs.

The Empress receives her new daughter-in-law in Schönbrunn. The relationship between the two women was by no means as intimate as suggested in this picture.

Marie Valerie — das Lieblingskind.

Marie Valerie — the favourite child.

Zeichnung Elisabeths für ihre Tochter.
A drawing by Elisabeth for her daughter.

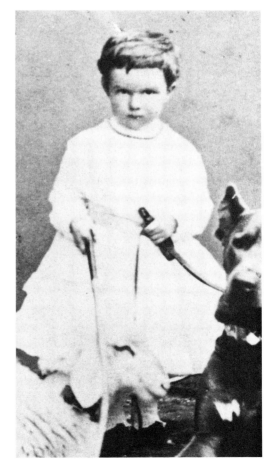

Früher als es ihr lieb war, wurde Sisi mit 36 Jahren Großmutter. Zur Taufe ihres ersten Enkelkindes (und Patenkindes), der kleinen Elisabeth (spätere Gräfin Seefried), reiste Sisi kurz nach München. Eine begeisterte Großmutter wurde sie nie.

At the age of 36 Elisabeth became grandmother — long before she wished to. On the occasion of the christening of her first grand-child (and God-child) Sisi travelled to Munich to see the small Elisabeth, the future Countess Seefried. She never became an enthusiastic grandmother.

Das Kaiserpaar 1879 mit den drei Kindern, dem Schwiegersohn Prinz Leopold und bereits zwei Enkelkindern (Elisabeth und Auguste von Bayern).

The Emperor and Empress in 1879 with their three children, son-in-law Prince Leopold and two grandchildren (Elisabeth and Auguste of Bavaria).

Weihnachtsabend in der Hofburg, 1887: das Kaiserpaar mit dem Kronprinzenpaar, Marie Valerie und der kleinen Erzsi (Zeichnung Wilhelm Gause).

Christmas Eve 1887 in the Hofburg: Emperor and Empress, the Crown Prince and his wife, Marie Valerie and the small Erzsi (drawing by Wilhelm Gause).

Sisi im so wenig geliebten Habsburger Familienkreis zur Zeit ihrer Silberhochzeit.

Sisi in the family circle she loved so little, on the occasion of her Silver Wedding Anniversary.

1. Kaiser Franz Josef.
2. Kaiserin Elisabeth.
3. Kronprinz Rudolf.
4. Erzherzogin Gisela.
5. Erzherzogin M. Valerie.
6. Erzherzog Franz Carl (†).
7. Herzog Philipp von S. Coburg.
8. Dessen Gemahlin Herzogin Luise.
9. Erzherzog Heinrich.
10. Erzherzogin Isabella (Friedrich).
11. Erzherzog Friedrich.
12. Kaiserin Charlotte von Mexiko.
13. Erzherzog Leopold.
14. Erzherzog Marie (Rainer).
15. Erzherzog Rainer.
16. Erzherzog Ludwig Victor.
17. Erzherzog Albrecht.
18. Erzherzog Wilhelm.
19. Erzherzog Ernst.
20. Erzherzog Sigismund.
21. Herzog Philipp von Württemberg.
22. Erzherzog Josef.
23. Erzherzogin Maria Theresia (Carl Ludwig).
24. Erzherzog Carl (Carl Ludwig).

use (1879).

...ogin Margarethe Sofie ... udwig).
...og Carl Ludwig.
...og Otto.
...og Franz Ferdinand

29. Königin Marie Henriette von Belgien.
30. Prinz Leopold von Bayern.
31. Erzherzogin Margarethe Clementine (Josef).

32. Erzherzogin Marie Christine (jetzt Königin Witwe von Spanien).
33. Erzherzogin Maria Theresia (Prinzessin Ludwig von Bayern).
34 u. 35. Kinder des Herzogs Philipp von Württemberg.

36. Erzherzogin Maria Theresia (Tochter des Erzherzogs Albrecht Gemahlin des Herzogs Philipp von Württemberg).
37. Erzherzogin Clotilde (Josef).

38. Erzherzog Ladislaus (Josef).
39. Erzherzogin Maria Dorothea (Josef).

Die Idylle vor dem Laxenburger Schloß, der Residenz des Kronprinzenpaares, täuscht: Zwischen diesen vier Menschen, Franz Joseph, Elisabeth, Rudolf und Stephanie, gab es so gut wie keinen Kontakt. Jeder lebte für sich allein.

This idyllic scene in front of Laxenburg Castle, the reside of the Crown Prince and his wife give a false impression. There was practically no contact between those four people. Franz Joseph, Elisabeth, Rudolf and Stefanie lived for themselves.

Wiener Zeitung.

Nr. 26.   Donnerstag, den 31. Jänner   **1889.**

Pränumerations-Preise: Für Wien ohne Zustellung: ... (Hauptbl. m. Amtsbl. u. „Abendpost") ganzj. 16 fl., halbj. 8 fl., viertelj. 4 fl. m. tägl. einmal. Zustellung: ganzj. 20 fl., halbj. 10 fl., viertelj. 5 fl., m. tägl. zweimal. Zustellung: ganzj. 22 fl., halbj. 11 fl., viertelj. 5 fl. 50 kr. Hauptbl. ohne Amtsbl. m. „Abendpost" ganzj. 12 fl., halbj. 6 fl., viertelj. 3 fl., m. tägl. einmal. Zustellung: ganzj. 16 fl., halbj. 8 fl., viertelj. 4 fl.; m. tägl. zweimal. Zustellung: ganzj. 18 fl., halbj. 9 fl., viertelj. 4 fl. 50 kr. — „Wiener Abendpost" allein ganzj. 4 fl., halbj. 2 fl., viertelj. 1 fl., monatl. 40 kr. — Mit tägl. einmal. Postversendung: Hauptbl. m. Amtsbl. u. „Abendpost" ganzj. 6 fl., halbj. 9 fl., viertelj. 4 fl. 50 kr. — Mit tägl. zweimal. Postversendung: Hauptbl. m. Amtsbl. u. „Abendpost" ganzj. 26 fl., halbj. 13 fl., viertelj. 6 fl. 50 kr. Hauptbl. ohne Amtsbl. m. „Abendpost" ganzj. 22 fl., halbj. 11 fl., viertelj. 5 fl. 50 kr. „Wiener Abendpost" allein ganzj. 6 fl., halbj. 3 fl., viertelj. 1 fl. 50 kr. — Auf das Amtsblatt allein findet keine besondere Pränumeration statt. — Die Pränumerations-Beträge sind franco an das Comptoir der Wiener Zeitung (1. Bezirk, Grünangergasse Nr. 1) einzusenden.

Amtlicher Theil.

Seine k. und k. Hoheit der durchlauchtigste Kronprinz Erzherzog Rudolph ist gestern, den 30. d. Mts., zwischen 7 und 8 Uhr früh in seinem Jagdschlosse in Meyerling bei Baden, am Herzschlag plötzlich verschieden.

Die erste Nachricht vom plötzlichen Tod des Kronprinzen Rudolf.

The first news of the sudden death of Crown Prince Rudolf.

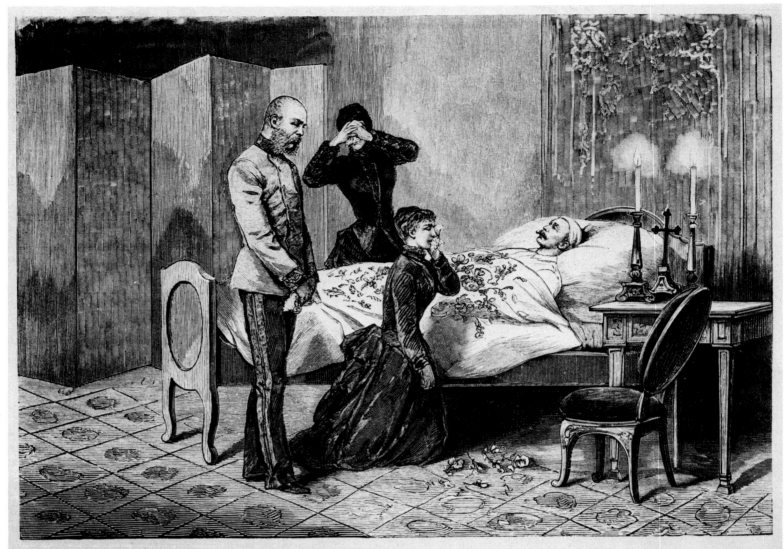

Phantasievolle Illustration für die Zeitungsleser: An der Bahre des 30jährigen Kronprinzen Rudolf weinen die Eltern und die Witwe.

A very imaginative illustration for the newspaper readers: parents and widow weep at the death bed of the 30 years old Crown Prince Rudolf.

Die Tragödie des Kronprinzen überraschte die Familie. Er erschoß sich am 30. Januar 1889 mit seiner jungen Geliebten Mary Vetsera in Mayerling.

The tragedy of the Crown Prince surprised the family. He shot himself and his young lover Mary Vetsera at Mayerling on January 30th, 1889.

Bei der Beisetzung ihres einzigen Sohnes in der Kapuzinergruft fehlte die Kaiserin. Ein Blumengesteck von ihr lag auf dem Sarg — neben dem der Kronprinzessin Stephanie.

At the funeral of her only son the Empress was not present. A wreath of flowers from her lay on the coffin — next to those of Crown Princess Stephanie.

Titanias Weltflucht

Titania's flight from the world

Seit den achtziger Jahren, als sie das Reiten wegen starker Gicht aufgeben mußte, beschäftigte sich die Kaiserin mit dem Verfassen von Gedichten nach dem Muster ihres Lieblingsdichters Heinrich Heine. Mehr denn je mied sie gesellschaftliche Veranstaltungen in Wien und das Zusammensein mit ihrem kaiserlichen Gatten. Sie fühlte sich als Feenkönigin Titania, als die sie sich auch in ihren Gedichten bezeichnet.

In the eighties, when the Empress had to give up riding due to severe gout, she occupied herself with writing poems in the style of Heinrich Heine, her favourite poet. More than ever she avoided the public eye and being with her Imperial husband. She imagined herself to be the fairy queen Titania and referred to herself as Titania in her poems.

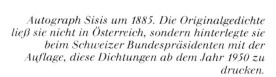

Autograph Sisis um 1885. Die Originalgedichte ließ sie nicht in Österreich, sondern hinterlegte sie beim Schweizer Bundespräsidenten mit der Auflage, diese Dichtungen ab dem Jahr 1950 zu drucken.

An autograph of Sisi's from around 1885. She didn't leave the original poems in Austria but left them in the care of the president of Switzerland on condition that they wouldn't be published before 1950.

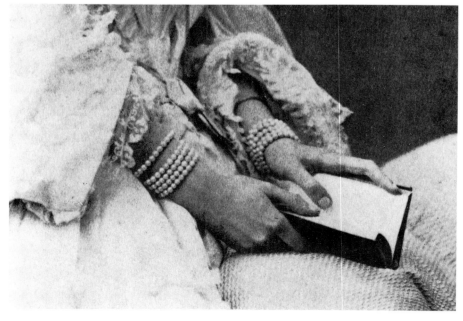

Den größten Teil ihrer späten Jahre verbrachte Elisabeth unter wechselnden Pseudonymen auf Reisen, vorzugsweise per Schiff. Vor allem liebte sie die griechischen Inseln. Sie lernte fließend Neugriechisch und lebte sich in die griechische Welt der Sagen und der Geschichte ein.

The greater part of her later years were spent travelling under different names. She preferred to travel by ship and especially loved the Greek islands. She learned to speek Greek fluently and became deeply involved in the work of Greek history and mythology.

Einer der wenigen Menschen, von denen sich Elisabeth verstanden fühlte, war ihr bayerischer „Königsvetter" Ludwig II. Beide verachteten die Menschen und die Politik, liebten die Einsamkeit und lebten in Phantasien.

One of the few people whom Elisabeth felt understood her was her Bavarian royal 'cousin', Ludwig II. Both despised people and politics, loved loneliness and lived in a world of phantasy.

Bild auf rechter Seite:
Elisabeths Prunk-Schlafzimmer in der Hermesvilla bei Wien mit Wandmalereien über Shakespeares Sommernachtstraum.

Picture on the right page:
Elisabeth's luxurious bedroom in the Hermes-Villa near Vienna with wall-paintings of Shakespeare's Midsummer Night's Dream.

Skizze von Leopold Horowitz aus Elisabeths letzten Jahren.

A sketch by Leopold Horowitz of Elisabeth in the last years of her life.

Für ihren Lieblingsdichter Heinrich Heine ließ Elisabeth bei ihrem Schloß Achilleion auf Korfu einen Tempel bauen.

Near Castle Achilleion on the island of Corfu Elisabeth had a temple built in honour of her favourite poet Heinrich Heine.

Dieses Gemälde des ungarischen Künstlers Horowitz entstand wie alle späten Porträts keineswegs nach dem lebenden Modell, sondern nach Fotos der jüngeren Kaiserin. Die Kaisertochter Marie Valerie fand, daß dieses Bild das beste ihrer Mutter war (Valerie-Tagebuch. 31. Dezember 1898). Wie Elisabeth wirklich in ihren letzten Jahren aussah, wissen wir nicht. Sie ließ sich weder fotografieren noch malen.

This oil painting by the Hungarian artist Horowitz was produced after seeing photos (like all the paintings of later days). The daughter of the Empress, Marie Valerie, was of the opinion, that this was the best of the pictures of her mother (see Valerie's diary, Dec. 31st, 1898). What Elisabeth really looked like in her last years is unknown. She did not allow herself to be photographed or painted.

Familiendiner mit den beiden Enkelsöhnen Georg und Konrad von Bayern. Die Kaiserin sitzt zwischen den Schwiegersöhnen Prinz Leopold von Bayern und Erzherzog Franz Salvator, der Kaiser zwischen seinen Töchtern Gisela und Marie Valerie (Zeichnung von Theo Zasche).

Family dinner with the two grandsons Georg and Konrad of Bavaria. The Empress is seated between her sons-in-law Prince Leopold of Bavaria and Archduke Franz Salvator. The Emperor is seen between his daughter Gisela and Marie Valerie (drawing by Theo Zasche).

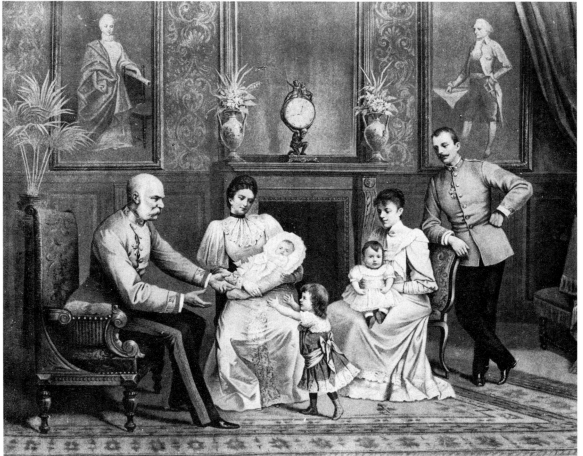

In rascher Folge wurde Marie Valerie neunfache Mutter. Hier das Kaiserpaar mit den ältesten drei Kindern Valeries, Ella, Franz und Hubert, und dem Schwiegersohn Franz Salvator 1894.

Valerie became mother of nine in a very short period of time. Here we see the Emperor and Empress in the year 1894 with Valerie's three eldest children: Ella, Franz and Hubert. On the right is the son-in-law Franz Salvator.

Links: Das alte Kaiserpaar, wie es sich die Illustratoren vorstellten.

Left: The old Imperial couple, as the illustrators imagined them.

Schnappschüsse aufdringlicher Fotografen in den neunziger Jahren.

Snapshots taken by obtrusive photographers in the nineties.

Das Kaiserpaar bei der Kurpromenade in Bad Kissingen.

The Imperial couple promenading at Bad Kissingen.

Elisabeth mit ihrer Hofdame Gräfin Irma Sztáray in Territet.

Elisabeth with her lady in waiting Countess Irma Sztáray in Territet.

Elisabeth beim Spaziergang mit der französischen Exkaiserin Eugénie (rechts) in Mentone.

Elisabeth walking with the former French Empress Eugénie (right) in Mentone.

Linke Seite:
Elisabeth mit einem ihrer griechischen Vorleser, Mr. Barker.

Left page:
Elisabeth with one of her reading companions for Greek, Mr. Barker.

The last festivity at the Imperial Court at which the Empress took part: cermonial dinner honouring the Russian Czar and his wife.

Patriotische Postkarte von der letzten Abfahrt der Kaiserin aus Wien.

A patriotic picture postcard showing the Empress' last departure from Vienna.

Visitkarte mit Elisabeths Pseudonym, das sie auch in Genf benützte: „Gräfin von Hohenembs".

A visiting card with Elisabeth's pseudonym which she also used in Geneva: „Gräfin von Hohenembs" (Countess of Hohenembs).

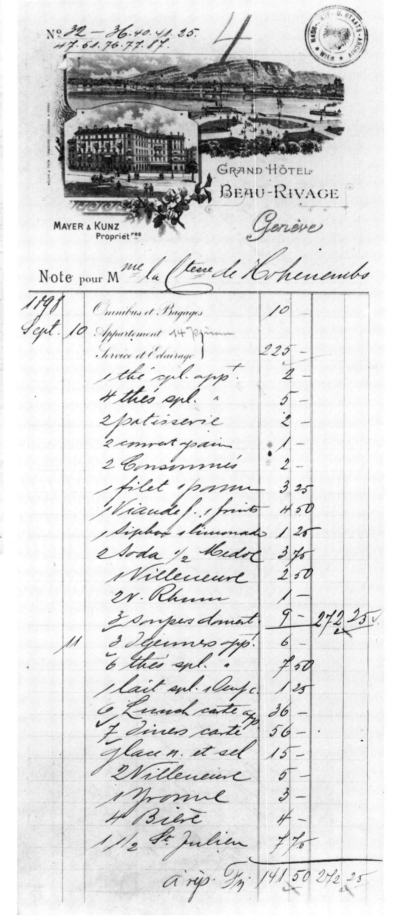

Letzte Speisekarte als Gast der Madame Rothschild in Pregny…

The last menu when Elisabeth was the guest of Madame Rothschild at Pregny…

… und letzte Rechnung für die „Comtesse de Hohenembs" im Hotel Beau Rivage.

… and the last bill for the 'Comtesse de Hohenembs' in the hotel Beau Rivage.

Wiener Tagblatt.

Demokratisches Organ.

Nr. 250.   Sonntag, den 11. September 1898.   48. Jahrgang.

Die Kaiserin ermordet!

Genf, 10. September, 3 Uhr 40 Minuten Nachmittags. Kaiserin Elisabeth verließ um 12 Uhr 40 Minuten Mittags das Hotel Beaurivage, um sich nach dem Landungsplatze der Dampfer zu begeben.

Auf dem Wege dahin stürzte sich ein Individuum auf die Kaiserin und führte einen heftigen Stoß gegen dieselbe. Die Kaiserin fiel zu Boden, erhob sich jedoch wieder und erreichte den Dampfer, wo sie bald darauf in Ohnmacht fiel.

Der Kapitän des Schiffes wollte das Schiff nicht abgehen lassen, gab indes später über Bitten des kaiserlichen Gefolges das Zeichen zur Abfahrt. Das Schiff hielt jedoch, nachdem es den Hafen verlassen hatte, wieder an und kehrte zum Landungsplatze zurück. Die Kaiserin hatte das Bewußtsein nicht wiedererlangt und wurde auf einer rasch hergestellten Tragbahre nach dem Hotel Beaurivage gebracht.

Die Kleider der Kaiserin zeigten Blutflecken.

Der Thäter wurde festgenommen.

Die Feile, mit der Elisabeth am 10. September 1898 vom Anarchisten Lucheni in Genf erstochen wurde.

The file with which Elisabeth was stabbed to death by the anarchist Lucheni in Geneva on September 10th, 1898.

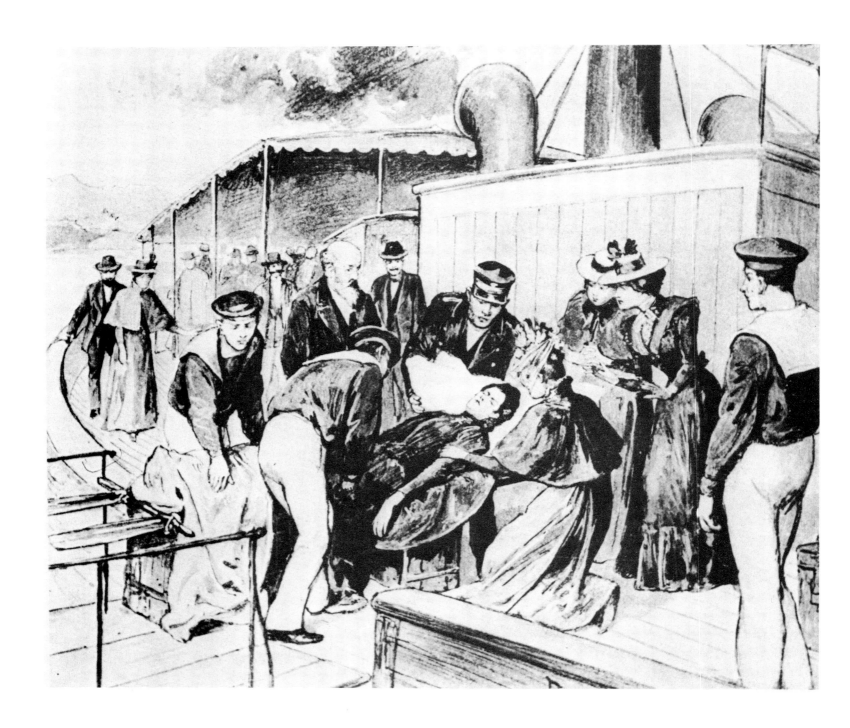

Nach der Tat konnte Elisabeth erstaunlicherweise noch einige Minuten von der Anlegestelle am Genfer See bis zum wartenden Dampfer gehen, ohne etwas vom tödlichen Ausmaß des Überfalles zu ahnen. Auf dem Schiff wurde sie ohnmächtig und starb. Jetzt erst enthüllte ihre Hofdame Gräfin Sztáray, daß diese als „Gräfin von Hohenembs" reisende fremde Dame die Kaiserin von Österreich war.

After the incident the Empress could surprisingly enough walk for a few minutes from the anchorage point at Lake Geneva up to the steamer without being aware of the deadly nature of the attack. It was on the ship that she fainted and died. Only now did her lady in waiting, Countess Sztáray, make it known that the foreign lady travelling under the name of 'Countess of Hohenembs' had been the Empress of Austria.

Plakette von Stefan Schwarz.

Engravings by Stefan Schwarz.

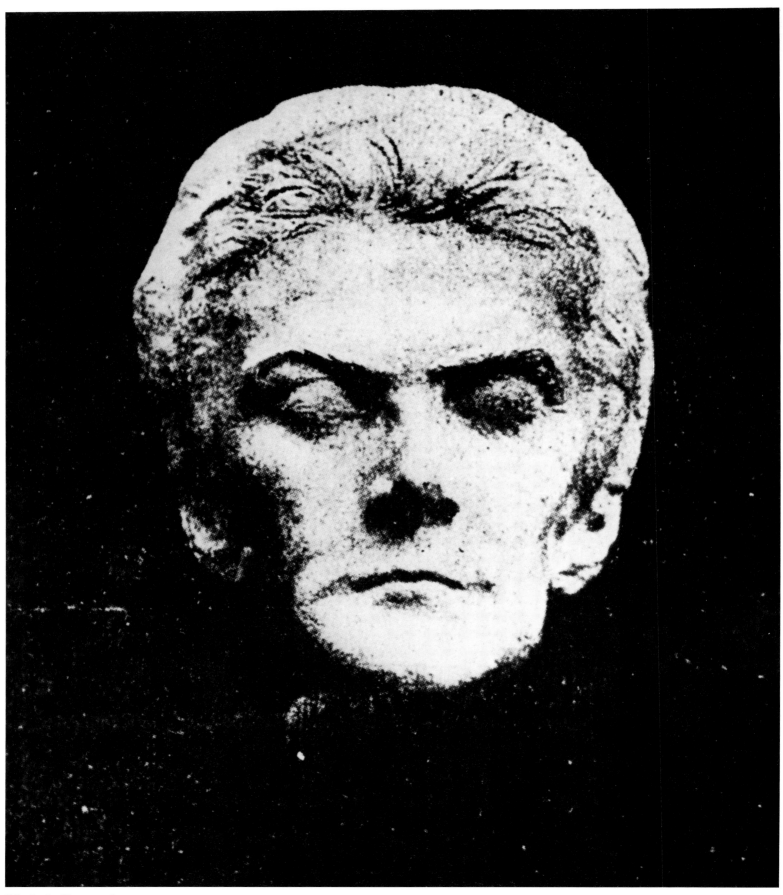

Elisabeths Totenmaske.
Elisabeth's death mask.

Der Kaiser empfängt Elisabeths Hofdame, Irma Gräfin Sztáray, in deren Armen die Kaiserin starb.

The Emperor receives Elisabeth's lady in waiting, Countess Irma Sztáray, in whose arms the Empress had died.

Gedenkpostkarte an Elisabeths Tod.

A picture postcard in remembrance of Elisabeth's death.

Zeitgenössische Illustrationen über die Beisetzungsfeierlichkeiten in der Kapuzinergruft.

Illustrations of the time showing the funeral ceremony in the Vienna Kapuzinergruft.

Volkstümliche Apotheose: Kronprinz Rudolf empfängt seine Mutter Elisabeth im Himmel.

Popular apotheosis. Crown Prince Rudolf receives his mother in heaven.

Kaiser Franz Joseph überlebte seine „Engels-Sisi" um 18 Jahre. Neben jedem seiner Schreibtische hing ein Elisabeth-Porträt (Gemälde von Franz Matsch).

Emperor Franz Joseph survived his 'Angel Sisi' by 18 years. Next to each of his desks one could see a portrait of Elisabeth (oil painting by Franz Matsch).

Bildnachweis

Österreichische Nationalbibliothek, Wien, Porträtsammlung:
16 (2), 19, 25, 27, 30, 31 u., 32 ob., 33, 34 (2), 35, 36, 37, 38 (2), 41, 29 (4), 30 (2), 33, 50, 51, 52, 59, 61, 62 (4), 63, 57 (4), 67 (2), 70 (3), 71, 73, 74 (3), 75, 76 (2), 77 (1), 78, 79 (1), 81, 82 (2), 84, 85, 87 (2), 88 ob., 89 (2), 90, 91 (2), 92 (2), 95, 98, 100, 101 (2), 108, 109, 110 u., 112 (2), 113 (2), 116, 117, 118, 120, 128, 129 u., 130, 132 (2), 135 (2), 138 (2), 139, 140 (2), 143, 144, 145 (3), 148 (3), 149, 150 (4), 151 (2), 154 (2), 155, 156/157, 158, 162 u., 164 (2), 169 (2), 170, 171 (3), 174 (2), 174 (2), 175, 182

Österreichische Nationalbibliothek, Druckschriftensammlung, zeitgen. Zeitungen:
23, 102 (2), 103, 104 (2), 105, 106 (2), 107 (2), 110 ob., 114, 115 (2), 119 (2), 123 (2), 124, 127, 141, 142 (2), 148 u., 159, 160, 161, 172, 175, 179 ob., 180 (2), 181 (2)

Kunsthistorisches Museum Wien (einschl. Kaiserappartements und Wagenburg):
16 ob., 21 u., 31 ob., 53, 54, 58, 93, 134
Historisches Museum der Stadt Wien:
24 (2), 40, 94, 120, 129 ob., 165, 166, 173, 183

Ehemaliges Hofmobilien- und Materialdepot Wien:
12, 13

Graphische Lehr- und Versuchsanstalt Wien:
28, 72 (3), 77 (2), 79 (4), 136 (3), 137 (3)

Haus-, Hof- und Staatsarchiv Wien:
26 u., 120 u.
Albertina: 39
Stift Göttweig: 16 u.
Zisterzienserstift Lilienfeld: 57
Joanneum Graz, Nachlaß Rosegger: 45
Museum der Stadt München: 8 (2), 10 u.
Geheimes Hausarchiv München: 14, 17, 22
Schweizer Bundesarchiv Bern: 162 ob.
Széchényi-Bibliothek Budapest: 178
Schloß Miramare bei Triest: 56, 122
Fürst Thurn und Taxis Regensburg: 55, 131
Gabrielle Gräfin Seefried: 29 (2), 31 (2), 60 (2), 64, 66, 68, 69, 70 (1), 74 (2), 83
Josef Korzer-Cachée, Wien: 111
Nischer-Falkenhof, Wien: 152 (6), 153 (5)
Dr. Herbert Fleissner, München: 15
Privat: 9 (3), 10 ob., 11, 20, 21 ob., 26 ob., 28, 29 (2), 44 ob., 48, 49, 76 (1), 80, 86 (2), 88 u., 96 (2), 97 (2), 99, 125 (2), 126, 133, 146, 147, 163, 167, 168 (3), 173, 176, 177, 179 u.